Companion Study Guide

SECRET
of the
SECRET
PLACE

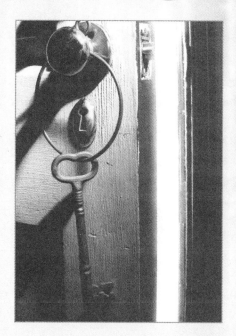

For Personal Reflection
& Group Discussion

Bob Sorge

Oasis House • Lee's Summit, Missouri

Second Printing (2005)

*SECRETS OF THE SECRET PLACE: COMPANION STUDY GUIDE
FOR PERSONAL REFLECTION & GROUP DISCUSSION*
Copyright © 2004 by Bob Sorge
Published by Oasis House
P.O. Box 127
Greenwood, Missouri 64034-0127

www.oasishouse.net

Contributing editor: Edie Veach.

Printed in the United States of America
International Standard Book Number: 0-9704791-8-2

Library of Congress Cataloging-in-Publication Data

Sorge, Bob
    Secrets of the secret place: companion study guide: for personal reflection & group
    discussion / Bob Sorge.
        p.cm.
    ISBN 0-9704791-8-2 (alk. paper)
        1. Sorge, Bob. Secrets of the secret place. 2. Prayer–Christianity–Meditations. I. Title

    BV210.3.S67 2004
    242'.–dc22

                                                                              2004043367

How To Use This Companion Study Guide

FOR PERSONAL REFLECTION

This section is for individual use. Groups have the option of discussing the items in this section, but they are designed primarily for personal contemplation.

1. Read the corresponding chapter in *Secrets Of The Secret Place*.

2. Respond to the questions. There are no right or wrong answers. Write your responses down—so you can return to the things you have journaled.

3. Focus on turning your responses into a conversation with God. Your studies in God's Word will always take you in three directions: things God wants you to believe; things God wants you to know; and things God wants you to do. Allow these three types of responses to draw you into closer intimacy with Him.

4. Use the "Notes" section to journal the thoughts that are really moving your heart. Be sure you always remember how God is speaking to you. You may even want to put a date by some entries.

FOR GROUP DISCUSSION

Bring this Guide with you to your small group meeting, together with your Bible and the text, *Secrets Of The Secret Place*. This study will have its greatest impact when you walk through it together with a small group of close friends who are fervently seeking to follow Jesus in the same way you are.

1. Choose a moderator to lead the discussion. (Optional: It can be a different person each time.)

2. Discuss the questions you find most relevant. The point is not to get through all the questions but to engage the group in lively interaction over the chapter's content.

3. Let's guard against "preaching" to one another. You will encourage your brothers and sisters most by speaking of your own pursuit of Jesus—both your successes and your frustrations. The goal is to help each other.

4. Use the "Notes" section to journal your gleanings during the discussion.

5. Before dismissing, offer your petitions to the Lord, together. Express your own desires to the Lord, and pray for other group members as the Lord seems to lead.

6. Homework: Read the next chapter and complete the section, "For Personal Reflection." Where and when is our next small group meeting?

1 The Secret of Saying "Yes"

*"He who dwells in the secret place of the Most High shall
abide under the shadow of the Almighty" (Ps. 91:1).*

For Personal Reflection

I CHOOSE TO BELIEVE

Read Phil. 4:13. What do you believe can change about your secret life with God?

"Reproductive power is unlocked in the shadow of the Almighty." Why do you believe that statement?

I DESIRE TO UNDERSTAND

Read Acts 10. As you look at the qualities of Cornelius's life, what role did the secret place have in his life?

How did God honor Cornelius as a result?

I RESOLVE TO RESPOND

What do you sense God specifically calling you to (as regards the secret place)?

Complete this sentence: "I'm saying YES, Lord, to…"

*The call of God burning in your breast will be uncontainable and unstoppable as you
devote yourself to the fiery passion of intimate communion with the Lover of your soul.*

For Group Discussion

CAN WE HELP EACH OTHER?

1. Do you default to watching TV when you need rejuvenation? How can we hold one another accountable?

2. Share an instance where time spent in secret with God was clearly the key to spiritual fruitfulness in your life or ministry.

3. How does the enemy condemn you for your failures? Perhaps others in the group can share ways they've dismantled accusations in their own lives. How does Jesus address accusation?

WE NEED HIS HELP

❖ Tell the group, as you approach the invitation before you, what the desire of your heart is. Then offer it as a prayer to God. Pause to see if any others in the group have a prayer of blessing to speak over you.

❖ Repeat this for each group member.

Notes

_____

_____

_____

_____

_____

_____

_____

_____

_____

_____

_____

_____

_____

_____

_____

As you devote yourself to the secret place with God, He will birth something within you that will spread, in His time, to the four corners of your sphere.

2 The Secret of the Shut Door

"But you, when you pray, go into your room, and when you have shut your door, pray to your Father who is in the secret place" (Matthew 6:6).

For Personal Reflection

I CHOOSE TO BELIEVE

Shut your door. Believe your Father is with you now. Talk to Him. How is He assuring you of His presence?

I DESIRE TO UNDERSTAND

Read Matt. 6:1-6; 16-18. What does the phrase mean to you, "your Father who sees in secret"? How does this speak to you about living for "an audience of One?"

Look at the usage of the word "place" in Gen. 28:10-19. Based on that passage, what might be the characteristics of the place where God meets with man?

I RESOLVE TO RESPOND

Read Matt. 7:24-27. Express to the Lord your resolve to establish godly foundations in your life. Tell Him of your determination to shut your door to the secret place. Is there one specific thing you intend to change, to safeguard that secret place?

The secret place is your portal to the throne, the place where you taste of heaven itself.

For Group Discussion

CAN WE HELP EACH OTHER?

1. Talk about your favorite place to meet with God. Are you able to get to the same place every day?

2. Look at Rev. 3:20 together. What are some of the ways you've opened the door of your heart to the Lord?

3. Talk about Jesus' emphasis on the secret place. How did He model getting alone with His Father?

4. Do you struggle to feel the Lord's presence in prayer?

WE NEED HIS HELP

In your prayer time together, let each one express his or her heart's cry to be aware of His presence. Agree together that He will lead each one of us into a more meaningful connection with Him.

Notes

_____

_____

_____

_____

_____

_____

_____

_____

_____

_____

_____

_____

_____

_____

_____

_____

*When you build your life on the blessed intimacy of a secret place
relationship with God, you are building on the rock.*

3 The Secret of Listening

"'My sheep hear My voice, and I know them, and they follow Me'" (John 10:27).

For Personal Reflection

I CHOOSE TO BELIEVE

Satan tries to convince you that you can't hear God's voice. Jesus, however, said that you can (John 10:27). Whom will you believe? Express your stand of faith regarding your ability to hear from God. (see Ps. 40:6)

I DESIRE TO UNDERSTAND

Read Isa. 66:1-4 carefully. Which truths from this passage are grabbing your attention most?

According to this Isaiah passage, what are some things that enable us to hear God's voice?

Using a Concordance (I urge you to purchase an exhaustive Concordance such as Strong's, or use a Bible search computer program—and use it frequently during your studies), look at the Scriptures where Jesus used the word, "hear." What did Jesus teach about the necessity of hearing? Note the verses that mean the most to you.

I RESOLVE TO RESPOND

Take 10 minutes to stop everything and just listen to God, in expectant faith. Make a note of your impressions.

What do you intend to do to make listening a regular part of your conversation with God?

Things don't change when I talk to God; things change when God talks to me.

For Group Discussion

3

CAN WE HELP EACH OTHER?

1. What in the "Personal Reflection" section was most meaningful to you?

2. Share with the group some things you're discovering in learning how to hear God's voice.

3. If you were to take Luke 8:17-18 as a promise rather than a threat, what would those verses mean to you?

4. How can we help each other become more disciplined listeners?

WE NEED HIS HELP

Use your group prayer time to listen together in quietness. Feel free to share, in 1-2 sentences, what the Holy Spirit seems to be impressing upon your heart. Is the Lord giving you a word of encouragement for anyone else in the group? Ask one person to close the time together by expressing our foremost request to the Lord.

Notes

_____

_____

_____

_____

_____

_____

_____

_____

_____

_____

_____

_____

_____

_____

_____

*The power of prayer is found, not in convincing God of my agenda,
but in waiting upon Him to hear His agenda.*

The Secret of Radical Obedience

"Whatever He says to you, do it"' (John 2:5).

For Personal Reflection

I CHOOSE TO BELIEVE

Of the four benefits of obedience listed in the chapter, which one is most important to you right now? What benefit do you believe your obedience will produce?

I DESIRE TO UNDERSTAND

Read Gen. 17, noting especially verse 23. Read Gen. 22:1-19, noting especially verse 3. What can we learn from Abraham's immediate, implicit obedience?

I RESOLVE TO RESPOND

Is there anything—even the tiniest thing—that you know He is asking of you, and yet you've hesitated? Take time to consider this carefully, and then when you're ready, write down what you intend to do in response, by His grace.

Radical obedience does not seek to comply to the minimal standards but pursues extravagant, lavish fulfillment.

For Group Discussion

4

CAN WE HELP EACH OTHER?

1. Beyond the four benefits listed in the chapter, what have you discovered to be a benefit of obeying God's word?

2. Discuss the closing statement of the chapter. Do you agree with the author? Why or why not? (You may want to look at Ex. 33:18-23.)

3. Tell the group if there's any area in your life in which you're deciding to invoke radical obedience.

WE NEED HIS HELP

Using Ps. 119:112 as a launchpad, let each one of you offer up your prayer to God, in the hearing of the group. Express the resolve of your heart, and call upon His mercy and grace.

Notes

_____

_____

_____

_____

_____

_____

_____

_____

_____

_____

_____

_____

_____

_____

_____

_____

_____

_____

The closer you get to God, the more important obedience becomes.

5 The Secret of Rapid Repentance

"Therefore if anyone cleanses himself…he will be a vessel for honor, sanctified and useful for the Master, prepared for every good work" (2 Tim. 2:21).

For Personal Reflection

I CHOOSE TO BELIEVE

Review Ps. 51:1-13. Look again at how David won God's favor by being a good repenter. Then read slowly through 1 John 1:6-9 and tell the Lord what you believe about each of those verses.

I DESIRE TO UNDERSTAND

Study the relationship between Rev. 3:18, 2 Tim. 2:19-21, and 1 Cor. 3:12-15. What are some other Scriptures that point to God's refining fires in our lives? How would you define the difference between wood and gold?

I RESOLVE TO RESPOND

Is there any way in which, through the crucifying of self, you can become a faster repenter? Express your heart to God. Take time today to calibrate your soul once again (take inventory). Don't move on until you sense His affections wrapping around you.

Ready repentance opens the channels for intimate communion with God.

For Group Discussion

CAN WE HELP EACH OTHER?

1. In what ways have you resisted repentance in the past? What have you learned about becoming a good repenter?

2. Tell of a time when the Lord showed you a subtle area of iniquity in your heart that you didn't see for a long time, but then He showed it to you so you could repent. How did the Lord reveal it to you? Did you feel His delight when you responded?

WE NEED HIS HELP

Let's each one of us confess our tendency to resist repentance and to justify ourselves. Then invite Him to reveal to us those areas in our lives that still displease Him, but of which we are totally unaware.

Notes

_____

_____

_____

_____

_____

_____

_____

_____

_____

_____

_____

_____

_____

_____

_____

_____

_____

_____

_____

Rapid repentance from iniquity will cause us to progress forward to more noble purposes in God's great house and will deepen our knowing relationship with Him.

6 The Secret of Sowing

"He who sows to the Spirit will of the Spirit reap everlasting life" (Gal. 6:8).

For Personal Reflection

I CHOOSE TO BELIEVE

Do you believe that investing time in the secret place will be honored and rewarded by God? Pray over this until you really believe it!

What do you believe about the power of God's seed (God's word) to effect change in your heart? Write down your conviction about the power inherent in God's seed.

I DESIRE TO UNDERSTAND

Linking 2 Cor. 4:1 & 16 with Luke 18:1-8, what principles can you glean from Jesus' parable about always sowing to the Spirit in prayer and not losing heart?

How does Ps. 126:5-6 apply to your life right now?

I RESOLVE TO RESPOND

With Gal. 6:7-9 open before you, express to God the resolve of your heart to sow to the Spirit.

Every moment you spend in the secret place is an investment.
You are investing into eternal realities.

For Group Discussion

6

CAN WE HELP EACH OTHER?

1. Can you think of a time you sowed into the secret place and later received a harvest? Tell your story.

2. Review together the parable of the sower, Matt. 13:3-9, 18-23. How does this parable speak to your desire to be fruitful spiritually? What can we do to get rid of the hardness, rocks, and thorns that hinder our hearts?

WE NEED HIS HELP

Are there any in our group who are feeling weary, and perhaps are even tempted to give up sowing to the secret place? Let's use our prayer time to pray specifically for those members who desire fresh momentum in their ability to devote themselves to God.

Notes

_____
_____
_____
_____
_____
_____
_____
_____
_____
_____
_____
_____
_____
_____
_____
_____
_____
_____
_____

It is impossible to sow to the Spirit without reaping a corresponding harvest.

7 The Secret of Refuge

"Be my strong refuge, to which I may resort continually" (Ps. 71:3).

For Personal Reflection

I CHOOSE TO BELIEVE

Do you really believe that God is your refuge—even when the storms seem to escalate around your prayer life? If so, worship Him now from Ps. 18:1-3. Affirm your confidence in God's protection.

I DESIRE TO UNDERSTAND

Read Ps. 91 carefully. List the things the Psalm says we can escape from as we flee to the secret place of the Most High.

Compare Ps. 91 with 2 Cor. 6:3-10, and write down your insights.

I RESOLVE TO RESPOND

My prayer: "I resolve, Lord, to run into You in times of distress. You alone are my strong tower. Teach me, Lord, how to hide in You." Make a note of those things you sense the Lord is putting in your heart right now.

There is a place where God hides His beloved—in the sanctuary of His presence.

For Group Discussion

7

CAN WE HELP EACH OTHER?

1. Have you, like Daniel and Jesus, ever been attacked while in the place of prayer?

2. See how Jesus, because He prayed, was able to go forth from Gethsemane to meet those arresting Him. He did not fall into temptation, as did the twelve disciples who slept instead of prayed. How does this speak to your life?

3. Describe how you've learned to find peace and rest in the midst of turbulence and storm.

WE NEED HIS HELP

Is anyone in the midst of a storm right now? Pray for peace in each other's lives, even in cases where the storm persists. Assure each other, through Scriptures and prayers, of the overshadowing wings of the Almighty. May we have grace to continually run into Him!

Notes

_____
_____
_____
_____
_____
_____
_____
_____
_____
_____
_____
_____
_____
_____
_____
_____

*Nothing can happen to you in the secret place that He
doesn't specifically allow for His higher purposes.*

8 The Secret of Decision Making

*"I will instruct you and teach you in the way you should go;
I will guide you with My eye" (Ps. 32:8).*

For Personal Reflection

I CHOOSE TO BELIEVE

Choose right now to believe that, according to Ps. 32:8-9, God is helping you to learn His will from the context of intimacy and proximity. Complete the sentence: "I believe God wants to reveal to me His will because…

I DESIRE TO UNDERSTAND

Compare 1 Sam. 28:5-8 (a passage about Saul) with 1 Sam. 30:7-8 (a passage about David). Both incidents happened pretty much simultaneously. What principles can you draw out from these passages, in order to know how to walk in the will of God? Why did God not guide Saul, and why did He guide David?

I RESOLVE TO RESPOND

Consider Col. 1:9 prayerfully. How are you determining to walk in the coming days, by His grace, so that He will reveal His will to you?

Jesus wants you making decisions from the fountainhead of intimacy with Him.

For Group Discussion

CAN WE HELP EACH OTHER?

1. How has this chapter confirmed for you the way to make important decisions? Do you have a story to share of a time when God led you?

2. Discuss whether or not you agree: The closer we draw to the Lord, the lesser our chances of making a wrong decision.

3. Talk about the thermometer/thermostat paragraph. Which are you? How can we become thermostats of society?

WE NEED HIS HELP

Use the language of Eph. 1:15-21 to pray for each other, that we might walk in the fullness of God's will.

Notes

_____

_____

_____

_____

_____

_____

_____

_____

_____

_____

_____

_____

_____

_____

_____

_____

_____

Intimacy precedes insight. Passion precedes purpose.
First comes the secret place, then comes divine guidance.

9 The Secret of No Plan B

"My soul, wait silently for God alone, for my expectation is from Him" (Ps. 62:5).

For Personal Reflection

I CHOOSE TO BELIEVE

Declare Ps. 108:12 to the Lord, "The help of man is useless." Then tell the Lord what you believe about His all-sufficient power. Confess the confidence of Daniel 3:17. You may want to sing a song to the Lord that declares He is enough.

I DESIRE TO UNDERSTAND

Study the life of King Asa, who knew the mighty delivering power of God (2 Chron. 14:9-13), but then years later when in distress, he did not turn to the Lord again for deliverance (2 Chron. 16, note especially verse 9). Look also at 2 Chron. 16:12. What strikes you most about Asa's example? Do you find 1 John 5:21 relevant here?

I RESOLVE TO RESPOND

Speak Ps. 57:7 to the Lord, "My heart is steadfast." Tell Him of the resolve of your heart to look to Him alone (Ps. 57:3). "Lord, I don't simply want relief from some other source, I want to see Your mighty salvation."

Our God loves to prove Himself strong on behalf of those who have no other gods before Him.

CAN WE HELP EACH OTHER?

1. What are some false gods that you have turned to in the past, for deliverance? Were you delivered?

2. Tell of a time when God delivered you.

3. Tell the group what resolve God has put in your heart as you have meditated upon the theme of this chapter.

WE NEED HIS HELP

Use Ps. 62:5-8 to express your hearts to the Lord. Call out for grace and mercy. Let each one express his or her prayer to the Lord, and let the others agree.

Notes

_____

_____

_____

_____

_____

_____

_____

_____

_____

_____

_____

_____

_____

_____

_____

_____

_____

_____

_____

_____

*When the storm hits, run into the secret place, establish your spirit, and
say to Him with unwavering resolve, "You alone are my expectation."*

10 The Secret of Burning

"Who makes…His ministers a flame of fire" (Heb. 1:7).

For Personal Reflection

I CHOOSE TO BELIEVE

Tell the Lord that you believe Jer. 23:29, that His word has the ability to set your cold heart on fire. Tell Him you're putting more confidence in His word than in the coldness of your heart. Will you believe that, like John the Baptist, you too can be a "burning and shining lamp?"

I DESIRE TO UNDERSTAND

Look up the word "fire" in a Concordance or Bible search program, and write down the Scriptures that are most striking to you.

Meditate upon James 4:5. In what ways do you believe the Holy Spirit yearns jealously over us?

I RESOLVE TO RESPOND

"Lord, I determine, by your grace, to stoke the fire of a burning heart by constantly returning to the secret place." Add another sentence of your own to that prayer.

When you draw close to the fire of God's word,
you are actually taking fire into your bosom.

CAN WE HELP EACH OTHER?

1. Read and discuss the second paragraph of Chapter 10. Does this paragraph articulate your current desires?

2. Compare Pro. 6:27-28 with Ez. 28:14. How can we take His fire into our bosom, and walk on hot coals? (talk about practical how-to's)

3. Have you learned any secrets of how to keep the fire burning continually in your heart, rather than being hot-cold-hot-cold?

WE NEED HIS HELP

Use the middle paragraph of page 39 to express your prayers to the Lord. Do you have the courage to pray this quotation? "Holy Spirit, let Your burning jealousy have its consuming way in my life, until every competing affection and false god is completely burned away and until one raging, all-consuming passion fills my entire being—love for the altogether Lovely One, the Man Christ Jesus!"

Notes

_____

_____

_____

_____

_____

_____

_____

_____

_____

_____

_____

_____

_____

_____

_____

_____

When you feel cold, distant, and "out of it" spiritually, it's time to retreat to the closet, place yourself before the fireplace of His word, and allow the intensity of His face to restore your fervency.

11 The Secret of Violence

"'The kingdom of heaven suffers violence, and the violent take it by force'" (Matt. 11:12).

For Personal Reflection

I CHOOSE TO BELIEVE

Meditate in Heb. 11:6 until it burns in your heart with fresh confidence. "I believe, Lord, that if I seek You diligently, You will reward me. Help me to be even more diligent!"

I DESIRE TO UNDERSTAND

Based on Heb. 12:1, what are some weights that could potentially slow down your race? What are some sins that would seek to trip you up?

Look at 1 Cor. 15:10 and 1 Tim. 1:14. Write down how His grace is at work in us to enable us to pursue Him with intensity. What is His role? What is ours?

I RESOLVE TO RESPOND

Cry out for grace. Write down the specific steps you desire to take to increase the intensity of your spiritual pace.

Swing your sword against the encroaching tentacles that seek to overgrow your secret life with God. Get alone with God, O man of violence! Kiss the Son, O woman of violence!

CAN WE HELP EACH OTHER?

1. Do you find yourself more zealous when within eyeshot of others than when alone with God (see p. 42, lower paragraph)? How is God changing you?

2. Talk about fasting—your struggles and breakthroughs. Has fasting helped you intensify your pursuit? Would your group want to plan a weekend of fasting together? Are there any other ways you can encourage each other in this grace of fasting?

WE NEED HIS HELP

Pray over each person in your group, one at a time. Ask for an impartation of grace, even as you lay hands in prayer upon one another. Contend for an increase of spiritual violence.

Notes

_____

_____

_____

_____

_____

_____

_____

_____

_____

_____

_____

_____

_____

_____

_____

_____

_____

_____

*One of the most violent things you'll ever do is wrestle down all
the competing elements in your calendar and consistently
carve out the time to shut yourself into the secret place.*

12 The Secret of Humility

*"And I will be even more undignified than this,
and will be humble in my own sight"* (2 Sam. 6:22).

For Personal Reflection

I CHOOSE TO BELIEVE

In what ways do you see yourself in Rev. 3:17? Tell the Lord about it. And then tell Him how much you believe Col. 2:9-10.

I DESIRE TO UNDERSTAND

Look closely at 1 Pet. 5:5-7 and James 4:6. What is God speaking to you about humility? In what ways do you see humility modeled by God Himself? (See Ps. 113:5-6 and Ps. 45:4.)

Spend some time in Isa. 57:15. God has chosen to manifest Himself to the humble. There are some paradoxes in this verse; what do you understand the verse to be saying? Write out your explanation of the verse.

I RESOLVE TO RESPOND

Prostrate yourself with 1 Tim. 1:17 open before you, and worship Him.

*The servant of God finds no greater joy than searching out ways
to humble himself in the presence of the Almighty One.*

CAN WE HELP EACH OTHER?

1. How do we walk in the tension of recognizing our own bankruptcy (Rev. 3:17) while at the same time acknowledging the richness of Christ's deposit in us (Col. 2:10)?

2. What are some ways you have learned to humble yourself before God?

3. Discuss this statement, "Prayerlessness is the first sign of prideful independence." How does this impact you?

WE NEED HIS HELP

In your closing prayer time, kneel together as you lift your prayers and worship to God. If there's room, prostrate yourselves before His greatness. Make yourself small, and make Him large.

Notes

_____
_____
_____
_____
_____
_____
_____
_____
_____
_____
_____
_____
_____
_____
_____
_____
_____

God dignifies us—with sonship, glory, acceptance, royalty, purpose—so that we might enjoy the highest privilege of casting it all at His feet.

13 The Secret of Intercession

"Therefore I exhort first of all that supplications, prayers, intercessions, and giving of thanks be made for all men" (1 Tim. 2:1).

For Personal Reflection

I CHOOSE TO BELIEVE

With your fingers at Hebrews 13:18-19 and 2 Peter 3:12, tell the Lord how you believe you have the ability, through intercession, to accelerate the coming of His kingdom.

I DESIRE TO UNDERSTAND

Look up the Scriptures listed in your Bible search program or Concordance for the words "intercessor" and "intercession." Write down the things God is teaching you about intercession.

Locate the verses in the New Testament where the apostles asked for the prayers of others on their behalf (e.g., Hebrews 13:18-19). How important was it to the apostles that other believers were standing with them in prayer and intercession?

I RESOLVE TO RESPOND

Choose three people to intercede for, and then jot them a brief note or email, telling them of your prayers on their behalf. Include a Scripture in your note to them.

Intercession is a response to pain.

CAN WE HELP EACH OTHER?

1. Discuss this statement, "One of the most profound ways you can love someone is by praying for him." Do you agree?

2. The book says, "Intercession is a response to pain." How have you learned to respond when you become aware of the pain of others in the body of Christ?

3. Got any secrets to share with the group on how to enter into effective intercession? (read James 5:16b)

WE NEED HIS HELP

Intercede together for some needs of people outside your group. Ask God to increase your effectiveness in intercession.

Notes

_____

_____

_____

_____

_____

_____

_____

_____

_____

_____

_____

_____

_____

_____

_____

_____

_____

_____

Intercession does something very powerful in the intercessor: it joins the heart of the intercessor to the heart of the one being prayed for.

14 The Secret of Watching

"'Take heed, watch and pray'" (Mark 13:33).

For Personal Reflection

I CHOOSE TO BELIEVE

Tell the Lord, "I know it's my responsibility to be alert and attentive in this hour." Confess your faith in His ability to make you quick to perceive. "I believe in the power of Your grace, Lord."

I DESIRE TO UNDERSTAND

Look at Matthew 26:41. There is a time to sleep and a time to pray. How can we know when it's time to stay awake in watchful prayer? (compare Mark 13:32-37)

Read Jer. 8:7 and Matt. 16:1-4. What were the signs the Pharisees had missed? Take inventory: Am I able to see what God is doing, or do I have to see something spectacular before I tune in?

I RESOLVE TO RESPOND

Cry to God for the Proverbs 2:3 ability to see and discern. In what specific way is God challenging you to watch and pray?

In the secret place, we do not hide from current events; rather we bring our awareness of current events to the searching lamp of the Scriptures and the Spirit of God.

CAN WE HELP EACH OTHER?

1. Obeying the exhortation of 1 Peter 1:13, what are some things we can do to be at the height of our mental powers in the secret place?

2. Do you ever pray with the newspaper or a news bulletin in front of you?

3. Look together at the bulleted points on page 53. Talk about the one that stands out most to you.

WE NEED HIS HELP

Pray together over current events in the church and world. Spend some time in quiet reflection, then talk about any impressions or insights you may be receiving about what God is doing in the earth today.

Notes

_____
_____
_____
_____
_____
_____
_____
_____
_____
_____
_____
_____
_____
_____
_____
_____
_____
_____
_____

*Those who watch, if they are attentive, may actually discern
the sound of Christ's coming.*

The Secret of Radiation Therapy

"For the Lord God is a sun" (Ps. 84:11).

For Personal Reflection

I CHOOSE TO BELIEVE

Do you believe that time in His presence changes you? Tell the Lord in your own words how much you believe this is true. Marvel at the power of His presence.

I DESIRE TO UNDERSTAND

Pray thoughtfully over 2 Cor. 3:18 and Heb. 10:19-22. What insights is God giving you about drawing close to Him?

Meditate on the radiation that exudes from God's glory. Can you think of any verses that give clarity to that truth? Start with 2 Cor. 3 and 2 Thess. 1:9.

I RESOLVE TO RESPOND

Is there an area of sin or weakness in which you desire greater victory? Strategize how you can expose your heart to radiation treatments—how you can spend extended periods of time exposing that area to God's presence. What's the plan?

When we place ourselves in the sun of His countenance, the radiation of His glory does violence to those cancerous iniquities that we often feel helpless to fully overcome.

For Group Discussion

CAN WE HELP EACH OTHER?

1. "Sin is like a cancer; God's presence is like radiation on that cancer." What does that statement mean to you?

2. Tell the group an area in your life you're wanting God to "zap" with His presence and glory. Make a note to follow up in two months' time to discover what God has done.

3. Tell a time when condemnation pushed you away from God's presence; and of a time when conviction drew you closer to God. What did you learn?

WE NEED HIS HELP

Split into pairs, and pray for each other. Pray for the Lord to lead each one into the triumph of Christ, especially in the areas that have been confessed.

Notes

_____

_____

_____

_____

_____

_____

_____

_____

_____

_____

_____

_____

_____

_____

_____

_____

_____

Now, through the blood of the cross, sinful man is able to come into the immediate presence of the holy God and subject himself to the glory that will change him.

16 The Secret of Time

"But as for me, my prayer is to You, O Lord, in the acceptable time" (Ps. 69:13).

For Personal Reflection

I CHOOSE TO BELIEVE

Establish yourself in the principle of 2 Corinthians 9:6. Tell the Lord you really do believe this: "The more time I spend with You, the greater the harvest I will enjoy."

I DESIRE TO UNDERSTAND

Go deeper with the statement, "When you neglect the secret place, He's not disappointed *in* you, He's disappointed *for* you." Pursue the truth that even in our weakness and immaturity and shortcomings we are desirable and delightful to God. We realize we are "dark, but lovely" (Song of Solomon 1:5), meaning that even though we are darkened by sin, we are still stunningly attractive to God. What other Scriptures do you want to note here?

I RESOLVE TO RESPOND

Tell the Lord how you are resolving to spend more time in His presence, and that you refuse to listen to the accuser's berating voice if you don't follow through perfectly.

Ready repentance opens the channels for intimate communion with God.

CAN WE HELP EACH OTHER?

1. What are your two primary hindrances to spending more time with your Lord in the secret place? Talk it around, addressing what can be done about it.

2. What kind of warfare do you face from the enemy when you try to devote yourself to the secret place

3. What time of day works best for your secret place?

WE NEED HIS HELP

Tell the group how much time you want to spend daily with the Lord over the next week. Ask them to pray for you right now about that.

Notes

_____

_____

_____

_____

_____

_____

_____

_____

_____

_____

_____

_____

_____

_____

_____

_____

_____

When circumstances or emotions are successful at robbing your secret place,
don't get guilty—get indignant!.

17 The Secret of Retreats

"My beloved spoke, and said to me: 'Rise up, my love,
my fair one, and come away'" (Song 2:10).

For Personal Reflection

I CHOOSE TO BELIEVE

Look at Jesus' prophecy in Luke 5:35. Was Jesus prophesying about you? Tell the Lord that you believe fasting from food and social interaction is your privilege as much as anybody's, and that His grace is sufficient to enable and empower you to do it.

I DESIRE TO UNDERSTAND

Which biblical characters spent extended time alone with God in fasting? Note their names, length of days, and a Scripture reference for your study. (Hint: start with Moses, Elijah, Daniel, Jonah, Jesus, Paul.)

What compelling qualities do you see in their lives as a result, to which you would aspire?

I RESOLVE TO RESPOND

Plan a fasting retreat. How many day(s) shall it last? What options can you pursue for a location? Which are your target dates? What will you bring?

Your secret life can be ignited into new levels with God through the strategic employment of prayer and fasting retreats at planned intervals throughout the journey.

For Group Discussion

CAN WE HELP EACH OTHER?

1. Have you ever done a fasting prayer retreat alone? What's your honest response when you think about the idea?

2. Do we feel strongly enough about this in our group to encourage each other to plan a personal retreat now?

3. Tell the others about any fears, misgivings, or insecurities you have arising in you. What are your reservations or hurdles to overcome? Let's talk about them together.

WE NEED HIS HELP

Pray for each one, regarding any insecurities or hurdles that were mentioned in question 3 above. Let's fight for each other in the Spirit, contending for new dimensions of break-through and blessing.

Notes

_____
_____
_____
_____
_____
_____
_____
_____
_____
_____
_____
_____
_____
_____
_____
_____
_____

Personal prayer retreats intensify and accelerate my pursuit of God.
They refresh and renew my weary spirit.

18 The Secret of Journaling

"Then He said to them, 'Take heed what you hear. With the same measure you use, it will be measured to you; and to you who hear, more will be given'" (Mark 4:24).

For Personal Reflection

I CHOOSE TO BELIEVE

Do you believe that if truth is to find a permanent home in your understanding that you're going to have to write it down? Tell the Lord what you believe about the necessity of journaling.

I DESIRE TO UNDERSTAND

Look up 2 Timothy 4:13. Do you think the "parchments" could have been Paul's collection of personal notes and journaled insights? Could this account for why they were so valuable to him? Do you see evidence in the Bible that any others had a practice of reviewing their collection of notes?

Starting with Psalm 119:11, which verses in Psalm 119 speak of retaining and clinging to God's word within our hearts?

I RESOLVE TO RESPOND

Write down the specific steps you intend to take to remember more clearly the insights you gain from God's word.

Make your journal the place where you chronicle the spiritual truths that quicken your spirit while you're in the secret place.

For Group Discussion

CAN WE HELP EACH OTHER?

1. Do you journal? If so, show an example to the others. If not, why not?

2. Discuss some of the different ways we might be able to journal. Is there a way of journaling that you know will work for your personality and lifestyle?

WE NEED HIS HELP

Pray for the power of retention. Ask God to bless and anoint each one's memory. Ask for mechanisms that will help us stay reminded of the precious truths from the Lord we don't want to lose.

Notes

_____

_____

_____

_____

_____

_____

_____

_____

_____

_____

_____

_____

_____

_____

_____

_____

_____

_____

I keep a journal for one simple reason: I am desperate for more!

19 The Secret of Meditating

"This book of Book of the Law shall not depart from your mouth, but you shall meditate in it day and night, that you may observe to do according to all that is written in it" (Joshua 1:8).

For Personal Reflection

I CHOOSE TO BELIEVE

Do you believe there is more richness in most Bible verses than you are currently able to see? If so, express to the Lord the longing of your heart for "the spirit of wisdom and revelation" (Eph. 1:17) to rest upon you mightily as you meditate in the word.

I DESIRE TO UNDERSTAND

Using a word search (computer program or Concordance), look up the words "meditate" and "meditation." Write out the verses that are most striking to you.

Choose one of those verses, and take 10 minutes to meditate in just that verse. Write your thoughts concerning that verse.

I RESOLVE TO RESPOND

If you want to make meditation a stronger part of your secret place, write down specifically how you want this to happen.

The only way to internalize good treasure is by squirreling it away diligently in the secret place of meditation.

CAN WE HELP EACH OTHER?

1. Choose a Scripture passage (before the group meets), then take it apart together using the questions in the middle paragraph of page 73. Then apply the points that are bulleted on page 74. If you have time, repeat these procedures with another passage.

2. Which insights gained in this exercise are you wanting to journal?

3. By doing this together, has this helped you see how to study and meditate in the Scriptures by asking questions?

WE NEED HIS HELP

Meditate silently together in the prayer of Colossian 1:9-11. Then, as individuals are so moved, let them lead out in one-sentence prayers that are the overflow of their meditation. It's okay if there are times of silence between prayers.

Notes

_____

_____

_____

_____

_____

_____

_____

_____

_____

_____

_____

_____

_____

_____

_____

_____

_____

_____

Once you come alive to the delight of meditating on God's word, you'll become addicted..

20 The Secret of Simultaneous Reading

"'By the mouth of two or three witnesses every word shall be established'" (2 Cor. 13:1).

For Personal Reflection

I CHOOSE TO BELIEVE

Meditate in Rev. 1:3 and 2 Tim. 3:16. Stay there until you find yourself desiring to read the Bible carefully, cover to cover.

I DESIRE TO UNDERSTAND

Read Heb. 1 & 2. Notice how the writer takes verses from different parts of Scripture and places them juxtaposed to each other, for effect. By doing this, how does Scripture help to interpret Scripture? Note the benefit of reading in several places simultaneously.

I RESOLVE TO RESPOND

Decide upon your own Bible reading plan. How can you read through the entire Bible in a way that works best for you? Write down the methodology of your plan.

I want every single portion of God's inspired word to have a chance at my heart.

CAN WE HELP EACH OTHER?

1. Share what your Bible reading practice has been. Have you had a systematic Bible reading plan? Have you been motivated to read through the entire Bible?

2. Evaluate the author's suggestion of simultaneous reading. What are the strong points and weak points of this approach? How would you improve upon this suggestion?

3. The author suggests that you read through the entire Bible annually. What's your response to that idea?

WE NEED HIS HELP

Pray for those who have lost momentum in their Bible reading. Agree with those who have fresh resolve to read systematically in God's word. And bless with your prayers those who prefer to read randomly and inspirationally—that whatever our approach, the word of God would have its full effect in our lives.

Notes

_____

_____

_____

_____

_____

_____

_____

_____

_____

_____

_____

_____

_____

_____

_____

_____

I want the full package, so I read the full package.

21 The Secret of Praying the Scriptures

"'In this manner, therefore, pray'" (Matt. 6:8).

For Personal Reflection

I CHOOSE TO BELIEVE

"I believe my Bible comprises _____ pages (enter the page count of your Bible) of prayer prompts. I can turn almost any Scripture into a prayer. God has given me language to approach Him in wisdom and faith." Allow the Holy Spirit to personalize this confession to your heart.

I DESIRE TO UNDERSTAND

Read Acts 4:23-31. Which Scripture did they pray back to God? How is verse 27 a direct reference to the quotation that is in verses 25-26? What was the Lord's response when they prayed this Scripture?

Can you find any other instances in the Bible where someone prayed over a Scripture? Make a note of them and their significance (e.g., Daniel).

I RESOLVE TO RESPOND

Tell the Lord of your resolve to pray to Him with biblical language. Ask His fire to be on your tongue. Take some time right now to pray to Him from the Scripture of your choice.

As we pray God's word back to Him, the language of His word becomes the working language of our daily dialogue with Him.

For Group Discussion

CAN WE HELP EACH OTHER?

1. Use your group time this week as a "clinic" to become freer in praying from the Scriptures. Choose a Bible passage. Read it together, and discuss the passage if necessary. Spend some time meditating quietly in the passage. Then begin to pray from that portion of Scripture. Let your prayers be short, one or two sentences in length at a time. Let each one follow another person's prayer, popcorn style. Let someone else's prayer trigger your prayers.

2. When the prayers cease, talk about what just happened. What did you learn? How can we become more fluent in this?

3. If you have time, do it all over again with another portion of Scripture. Continue as long as time permits.

WE NEED HIS HELP

Close by asking the Lord to help each one of us to grow in this grace of praying with biblical language.

Notes

_____

_____

_____

_____

_____

_____

_____

_____

_____

_____

_____

_____

_____

_____

_____

_____

We want God's word to enter our hearts, grab our attention with its impact, enlarge and expand our hearts with passionate longing, enter into the fabric of our speech and actions, and bear fruit unto eternal life.

22 The Secret of Finishing

"'Do not be hasty to go from his presence'" (Eccl. 8:3).

For Personal Reflection

I CHOOSE TO BELIEVE

Look at 1 Sam. 21:7. Tell the Lord you believe He has the right to detain you in His presence for as long as He might desire.

I DESIRE TO UNDERSTAND

Read Exo. 24:12. When God called Moses to the mountain, did He tell him it would be for 40 days? What does it mean for your life that sometimes God says, as He did to Moses, for you to simply "be there"?

Meditate in Eccl. 8:3. Note the things coming to mind as you consider this verse. How might we know when the King has given us the release to move on to the next thing?

I RESOLVE TO RESPOND

Write down how you sense the Holy Spirit is challenging you about letting Him decide when the time is finished. Is there something specific you plan to change about the time you make available to the secret place? Wait attentively in His presence until He releases you.

Having come into His presence boldly through the blood of Christ,
let us not be hasty to leave.

For Group Discussion

CAN WE HELP EACH OTHER?

1. If God wanted to detain you longer, would He have that prerogative with you? Have you built any flexibility mechanisms into your secret place that would help you respond if God so called?

2. Since reading this chapter, have you tried asking the Lord, "Are you finished with me yet?" How did you know when the time was truly finished?

WE NEED HIS HELP

Worship Him together as the King, even over your small group. Minister to Him, give Him your praise and love. Stay there till He's finished with you.

Notes

_____

_____

_____

_____

_____

_____

_____

_____

_____

_____

_____

_____

_____

_____

_____

_____

_____

_____

_____

Let God decide when it's over. Give Him the honor of dismissing you.

23 The Secret of the Morning

"Now in the morning, having risen a long while before daylight, He went out and departed to a solitary place; and there He prayed" (Mark 1:35).

For Personal Reflection

I CHOOSE TO BELIEVE

Write down what you believe Jesus' example in Mark 1:35 speaks to your life.

I DESIRE TO UNDERSTAND

Applying the term "the womb of the morning" (Psalm 110:3) to the secret place, what are the implications of that term for your personal secret place?

Doing a word search (computer or concordance), look up the verses that have "firstfruits" in them. If our secret place is a firstfruits of our best energies to God, what principles from these verses give you further instruction regarding the secret place?

I RESOLVE TO RESPOND

What is your best time of day? What are you determined to do to give Jesus your best?

Even when His body craved more sleep, Jesus knew His true source of revitalization would not be on His back but on His face.

For Group Discussion

CAN WE HELP EACH OTHER?

1. Do you have a set time and place when you meet with God? What has been working best for you recently?

2. Talk about the time of day that works best for you. What have you learned about your body clock? Have you learned any tricks that enable you to be the most alert possible?

3. For those in our group who are not "morning people": Do you push yourself to go to the secret place in the morning anyways? Or do you choose another time of day instead?

4. David said, "I will awaken the dawn" (Psalm 108:2). How do you feel about that statement?

WE NEED HIS HELP

Ask each person: After our discussion today, what is your foremost request of God? Going in a circle, let each person pray aloud (one at a time) for the person on his or her left, especially regarding this request.

Notes

_____

_____

_____

_____

_____

_____

_____

_____

_____

_____

_____

_____

_____

_____

_____

_____

Give Him the portion of your day that works best for your personality.

24 The Secret of Getting Dressed

"Put on the whole armor of God, that you may be able to stand against the wiles of the devil" (Eph. 6:11).

For Personal Reflection

I CHOOSE TO BELIEVE

Meditate for a while in 2 Pet. 1:3. Give thanks that He has equipped you with everything you need to resist the devil. Rejoice in the fearlessness with which you enter the battle.

I DESIRE TO UNDERSTAND

Why does the warfare escalate as soon as we turn toward the face of God (Rev. 12:10)? Write the reasons.

Look at Isaiah 59:17, 1 Thess. 5:8, and any similar verses. How does a believer clothe oneself with these garments?

I RESOLVE TO RESPOND

What can you do to clothe yourself with spiritual armor before the enemy assails you? What specific steps is the Lord showing you to take, to be better prepared for the warfare?

Jesus is your every article of clothing.

CAN WE HELP EACH OTHER?

1. What are the primary accusations the members of the group face from the enemy? Take time together to ferret out some Scriptures we can use as a shield against these accusations.

2. Share how you personally have learned to put on each piece of the armor of God.

WE NEED HIS HELP

Go through Eph. 6:11-18 as a group. Take time to prayerfully put on each piece of the armor of God. Persist until you know Christ clothes your entire being. Then, once we're all dressed, let's spend some time in prayer and supplication (since this is the purpose of getting dressed). Let's exercise the spiritual authority we now enjoy and enforce Christ's reign in the earth through prayer.

Notes

_____

_____

_____

_____

_____

_____

_____

_____

_____

_____

_____

_____

_____

_____

_____

_____

_____

_____

_____

When we realize we're clothed in Christ, our confidence level
before God soars to the heavens.

25 The Secret of Self-Denial

"Then Jesus said to His disciples, 'If anyone desire to come after Me, let him deny himself, and take up his cross, and follow Me'" (Matt. 16:24).

For Personal Reflection

I CHOOSE TO BELIEVE

Do you perceive Jesus' invitation to self-denial as something to dread and endure, or as something to invoke with anticipation because of what is being offered? Write down what you believe about self-denial.

I DESIRE TO UNDERSTAND

When Jesus invited the rich young ruler to sell all and follow Him, all he could see was the pricetag. But what was the invitation Jesus was offering Him? (Matthew 19:16-22) Does He extend the same invitation today to those whom He calls to sell all?

Look at John 17:19 and its context. In what ways did Jesus sanctify Himself? What does that mean for us—how can we also sanctify ourselves?

I RESOLVE TO RESPOND

What are some areas of self-denial that you believe God desires to be part of your future walk with Him? What do you sense His grace empowering you to embrace in the here and now? Is your love awakening in anticipation? What is your next step?

Self-denial and intimacy go hand in hand.

CAN WE HELP EACH OTHER?

1. Besides the four listed in the chapter, what other benefits do you see of self-denial?

2. For self-denial to be effective, it must be done in love for Christ. How can we grow in loving expressions of self-denial without getting into legalistic bondage?

3. Tell of a way in which you denied yourself, and how it became a portal to great blessings in your life. Did you feel closer to Jesus?

WE NEED HIS HELP

Ask the group: Are there any areas of self-denial that you know the Lord is calling you to, but for which you deeply realize your need for more grace from above? Let's come to the Lord humbly for these things and receive grace to help in our time of need.

Notes

_____

_____

_____

_____

_____

_____

_____

_____

_____

_____

_____

_____

_____

_____

_____

_____

_____

_____

The more you deny yourself, the more the scales fall from your eyes.

26 The Secret of Boredom

"Watch and pray, lest you enter into temptation. The spirit indeed is willing, but the flesh is weak'" (Matt. 26:41).

For Personal Reflection

I CHOOSE TO BELIEVE

Declare: "I believe that Jesus is bigger than my boredom. I believe the pursuit of God carries the potential of unparalleled exhilaration. I believe God is strengthening my faith in what He has in store for me, to empower me to press past the boredom threshold into the joys beyond that await me."

I DESIRE TO UNDERSTAND

Look up John 14:16, 26; 15:26; 16:7. How would you describe the Holy Spirit's ministry in relation to the saints? How might we access the Holy Spirit's help?

Who are some people in the Bible who fell asleep? (Suggestion: look in your concordance for words like sleep, slept, asleep.) Was spiritual boredom ever a factor? What other factors were involved? What lessons are you learning about boredom?

I RESOLVE TO RESPOND

What are some areas of self-denial that you believe God desires to be part of your future walk with Him? What do you sense His grace empowering you to embrace in the here and now? Is your love awakening in anticipation? What is your next step?

Allow nothing to dissuade or detour you, boredom included.

For Group Discussion

CAN WE HELP EACH OTHER?

1. Do you fight sleepiness in the secret place? Do you tend to berate yourself when it happens? How can we be established in grace and mercy, even when we're caught by the weakness of our bodies?

2. Talk about this statement: "The more you persevere in the secret place, the very nature of your relationship with the Lord begins to change—and the bad days get fewer and further inbetween!" Have you found this to be your experience?

3. When we're bored out of our skull and have the choice to persevere in the secret place or revert to another distraction that will alleviate our boredom (such as a visit with a friend or a means of entertainment), what can we do to make the right choice?

WE NEED HIS HELP

Let's be honest with the Lord. Let's confess our boredom, and whatever tendencies we have to satisfy the boredom rather than push past it. Then, let's call together upon our Helper, the Holy Spirit. Call out to the Lord on behalf of one another. Let's fight together for a greater dimension of victory.

Notes

_____

_____

_____

_____

_____

_____

_____

_____

_____

_____

_____

_____

_____

_____

_____

One day of exhilaration in the Holy Spirit is worth a thousand days of struggle.

27 The Secret of Feeling Attractive to God

"So the King will greatly desire your beauty;
because He is your Lord, worship Him" (Ps. 45:11).

For Personal Reflection

I CHOOSE TO BELIEVE

Meditate in Hebrews 10:19-22. Let the reality of the "in" you have with God impact the depths of your understanding. Then go to Song of Solomon 4:7-11, and listen as He speaks every phrase over your life. Agree with what He says about you. Believe Him!

I DESIRE TO UNDERSTAND

Read Psalm 45. Write down every aspect of the way in which Christ views us, His beloved Bride.

Why has God made humans with the longing to be desired by another? What happens within us when He tells us He desires us?

He is your Father and you are His child. How does He, as Father, view you—even when you're still childish or immature? Which verses substantiate this best for you?

I RESOLVE TO RESPOND

When the enemy begins to demean you and tell you you're unlovely, what will your response be? Which scriptural truths will best extinguish his flaming arrows aimed at your heart?

When you come to the secret place, you are coming into the chambers of
the King who finds you both beautiful and desirable.

For Group Discussion

CAN WE HELP EACH OTHER?

1. Before coming to this week's discussion, spend some time in personal prayer for the others in the group, and bring a Scripture for at least one other group member, to encourage that person in the affections of Christ for him or her.

2. Tell the group how you usually feel God views you. In what way is the Lord renewing your mind? Are you coming to see God in a new way?

3. Share conversationally about how the cross has forever changed how God looks at mankind. Which truths or Scriptures about Christ's shed blood are most precious to you? How have you learned to receive the sprinkling of Christ's blood in your life? (1 Peter 1:2)

WE NEED HIS HELP

Offer the prayer of Ephesians 3:17-19 over each other—that we might be rooted and grounded in the awesome love of Christ. Here's one way to do that: Choosing each person one at a time, let the others in the group speak their prayers of blessing aloud over each one, putting into their own words the meaning of the Ephesians 3 prayer. We're contending for each other to be established in love. Let the words of your prayers wash one another and administer the grace of Christ's love.

Notes

_____
_____
_____
_____
_____
_____
_____
_____
_____
_____
_____
_____
_____

You are stunningly beautiful to Jesus!

28 The Secret of Desperation

"When she heard about Jesus, she came behind Him in the crowd and touched His garment" (Mark 5:27).

For Personal Reflection

I CHOOSE TO BELIEVE

"Lord, I am choosing to believe that the circumstances in my life which I don't understand are, in fact, designed by Your kindness to bring me into spiritual desperation. Thank You for loving me enough to direct my heart to something higher in You." Add your own words to this statement of faith.

I DESIRE TO UNDERSTAND

Read the story of the siege of Samaria, 2 Ki. 6-7. When you see the dire conditions of the siege, what characteristics or qualities of desperation are you able to see? (For example, "Desperation produces a change of values.")

Do you see some of the same characteristics in the story of the woman in Mark 5:25-34?

Job called himself a "desperate one" (Job 6:26). How did God produce desperation in Job's life? (see Job 1-2) What was the result? (Job 38-42)

I RESOLVE TO RESPOND

If you have been made desperate by God, write out the resolve of your heart to pursue Him with utter abandonment. Or if you're wanting to be made desperate, write out your prayer to Him.

Desperation will turn you into a different person.

CAN WE HELP EACH OTHER?

1. How would you rate your current comfort level? Is your life reasonably orderly and routine—or is it more out of control and desperate? What relationship would you say exists between your comfort level (or lack thereof) and your level of spiritual hunger?

2. Are desperate people easily misunderstood? Has there been a time when your zeal for God has been misunderstood? (Compare Psalm 69:9.) Or have you ever looked at others in distress and been critical of how they're walking the thing out?

3. How have you learned to walk with God in seasons of intensity or pain? Got any suggestions for the rest of us?

WE NEED HIS HELP

Look at the "dangerous prayer" in the middle paragraph of page 115. What kind of dangerous prayer are you ready to offer to the Lord? Let's do it together. Take time to hear each other's prayers, and bless each other with agreeing prayers.

Notes

_____

_____

_____

_____

_____

_____

_____

_____

_____

_____

_____

_____

_____

_____

_____

_____

_____

Hardship produces desperation, which in turn produces intense intimacy.

The Secret of Manna Gathering

*"The person who labors, labors for himself,
for his hungry mouth drives him on" (Pro. 16:26).*

For Personal Reflection

I CHOOSE TO BELIEVE

Read Matt. 4:4, and then tell the Lord what you believe about that verse. Express to Him that He is your very life and survival. Express your confidence in the power of His word to satisfy every craving and need of your heart.

I DESIRE TO UNDERSTAND

Read Exodus 12:16-31. What are some principles you see regarding manna-gathering that are relevant to your life?

Write out approximately 5-10 verses from Psalm 119 that stir your appetite to pursue the food of God's word.

I RESOLVE TO RESPOND

Resolve to make this your daily cry, "Give us this day our daily bread." Are you determined to pursue feeding yourself daily in the word of God until the secret place becomes your primary source of sustenance? Tell the Lord what you're after, and receive grace to go digging.

*Spiritual hunger is absolutely essential to spiritual health because without it
we won't be motivated to feed on the manna of God's word.*

For Group Discussion

29

CAN WE HELP EACH OTHER?

1. The chapter makes the connection between a loss of hunger and sickness. Talk about your own level of spiritual hunger. Are you working with any inner sicknesses, or are you sickness-free?

2. Talk about the elements listed at the bottom of page 117 for restoring one's spiritual appetite. Which have you proven to be effective in your life?

3. The author writes, "It's not that difficult to learn how to gather manna. Just get out there and start working. Pick up your Bible, and begin to labor in it." "No man is to teach you how to find this knowing relationship with God; the Holy Spirit Himself will be your teacher." Is the author right, or overly simplistic?

WE NEED HIS HELP

Express any insecurities, fears, or frustrations you feel about feeding yourself in the word. Then pray for each other. Let's really fight for each other in the Spirit, for a divine breakthrough in this area. Pray for each one to be made alive to the power of God's word.

Notes

_____
_____
_____
_____
_____
_____
_____
_____
_____
_____
_____
_____
_____
_____
_____
_____

Learn to gather your own manna. Then you'll have something to share.

30 The Secret of Enduring

"You therefore must endure hardship as a good soldier of Jesus Christ" (2 Tim. 2:3).

For Personal Reflection

I CHOOSE TO BELIEVE

Read Matt. 10:22 and 24:13. Also look again at what the author says about Col. 1:11 (page 122). Tell the Lord what you believe about endurance and the necessity of endurance to the success of the Christian life.

I DESIRE TO UNDERSTAND

Sometimes, we may endure in the word for many days without seeing any significant results. Perhaps it's like gardening. A gardener doesn't see his garden responding immediately to his labors (see Mark 4:26-29). What truths about gardening might encourage you to continue to endure in the word?

Look at Rom. 15:4. In what ways would you say the Scriptures are patient?

I RESOLVE TO RESPOND

There is nothing the enemy will resist more than a commitment to endure in faith and love. Prepare yourself for the war. Tell the Lord how you are purposing to endure in the secret place, and express your confidence in Him that He will bring you to the finish line.

The longer the distress, the more valuable the pearl.

30

For Group Discussion

CAN WE HELP EACH OTHER?

1. Some Christians say, "Don't ask for patience, you might not like what you get." Do you agree with this line of thinking?

2. The more Jesus hurt, the harder He prayed. How does His example speak to you?

3. Talk about this statement, "There is nothing else that changes us quite so readily and profoundly as a devotion to the secret place in the midst of grueling hardship."

4. Would you say you're in an "endurance mode" right now?

WE NEED HIS HELP

This chapter closes by pointing to the revelation of God that John was granted as he endured in the Spirit in the midst of hardship. Do you carry a similar passion and hope for a personal visitation of Jesus Christ to you? Ask the Lord together for grace to persevere, and call upon Him to visit you with His power and glory.

Notes

_____
_____
_____
_____
_____
_____
_____
_____
_____
_____
_____
_____
_____
_____
_____
_____
_____

The sanctuary of His embrace is where God reveals purpose, which in turn empowers us to endure hardship with joy for we know He is working it all together for good.

31 The Secret of Confinement

"You have hedged me behind and before, and laid Your hand upon me.
Such knowledge is too wonderful for me; it is high, I cannot attain it" (Ps. 139:5-6).

For Personal Reflection

I CHOOSE TO BELIEVE

Will you dare to believe that God has imprisoned you with purpose? Consider Luke 22:31-32. Do you believe that Jesus will pray you through this thing? Express your faith and confidence in God's sovereignty in your life.

I DESIRE TO UNDERSTAND

Look at Ps. 87:7. What does it mean to have all our springs (or fountains) in Him? In what ways would you say the Lord is your only source of refreshment or renewal? Did He confine you to enlarge your understanding?

Are you in any kind of prison for the Lord's sake? Consider Ps. 69:33 and its context. What is the Lord showing you about your prison or season of confinement?

Look again at Joseph's story, Gen. 37-46. How did God use Joseph's confinement as a place of secret encounter with Him? How did Joseph change?

I RESOLVE TO RESPOND

How is the Lord inviting you to respond to your chains? Are you willing to see this prison as an invitation to a greater intimacy? Tell Him how you are positioning your heart for the race set before you.

When the lights of understanding go out and you're plunged into emotional darkness,
you are actually being issued an invitation into God's secret place.

31

For Group Discussion

CAN WE HELP EACH OTHER?

1. What are some specific areas of confinement in your life—ways you are hindered from full freedom or movement, against your will? What do you see as the Lord's purpose for these chains? Encourage one another.

2. Have you ever been in a season of no options? Have you, like David in Ps. 139:5-6, viewed that time as the Lord's wonderful affections bestowed upon you?

3. Talk about social isolation and loneliness. How have you learned to persevere through such times?

4. How can we transform our seasons of confinement into seasons of encounter?

WE NEED HIS HELP

Use the prayer time to minister to those in the group who are in a place of confinement. Don't preach to them with your prayers. Rather, speak grace and blessing to them. And believe for the chains to be broken in the fullness of God's time.

Notes

_____

_____

_____

_____

_____

_____

_____

_____

_____

_____

_____

_____

_____

_____

_____

_____

He imprisons those He loves in order to awaken them
in the secret place to mature bridal affections.

The Secret of Waiting

*"For since the beginning of the world men have not heard nor perceived
by the ear, nor has the eye seen any God besides You,
who acts for the one who waits for Him" (Isa. 64:4).*

For Personal Reflection

I CHOOSE TO BELIEVE

Renew yourself in Isa. 40:28-31. Why is God asking you to wait upon Him? Write those things down; then declare your confidence in His good purposes for your life. Let the Lord speak Isa. 49:23 to your heart.

I DESIRE TO UNDERSTAND

The 14th verse of Ps. 27 is the capstone on an incredible Psalm. Read the entire Psalm in light of verse 14, and notate the insights you see throughout Ps. 27 regarding waiting on God.

What do you believe Ps. 69:6 means? Turn the verse into your own prayer.

Study Ps. 106:13-15. Look at the passage in light of the phrase, "They did not wait for His counsel" (v. 13). What do we risk when we are impatient? Write out your insights on waiting from this passage.

I RESOLVE TO RESPOND

Consider Col. 1:9 prayerfully. How are you determining to walk in the coming days, by His grace, so that He will reveal His will to you?

*Here's what God does with His ministers who wait on Him:
He makes them a flame of fire!*

32

For Group Discussion

CAN WE HELP EACH OTHER?

1. Talk about this quotation: "There is no frenetic hurrying in heaven, only calculated purpose." What does that phrase mean for you?

2. What is the difference between waiting for God and waiting on God? How do we do the latter?

3. It is proper for servants to wait upon their King. Have there been times when, instead of waiting on God for His opportune moment, God has had to wait on you for you to find an opportune moment for Him? Do we sometimes get this thing backwards?

WE NEED HIS HELP

Let's use our prayer time this week to simply wait upon the Lord. Gaze upon Him. Love Him. Sit in silent attentiveness. And do it together. Stand before Him as His attendants for as long as time allows. Let your thoughts be just for yourself and Him.

Notes

_____

_____

_____

_____

_____

_____

_____

_____

_____

_____

_____

_____

_____

_____

_____

_____

_____

_____

To wait on God successfully, we must come to derive more fulfillment

33 The Secret of Tears

"Put my tears into Your bottle" (Ps. 56:8).

For Personal Reflection

I CHOOSE TO BELIEVE

Do you believe that God stores and remembers your tears (Ps. 56:8)? Tell the Lord what you believe about the power and purity of tears, and of your openness to this expression.

I DESIRE TO UNDERSTAND

Read Luke 7:36-48. What role do tears play in this story? Would the story be the same without them? What did this woman touch of spiritual reality through her tears?

See the role that tears played in Hannah's story (1 Sam. 1:10 and surrounding verses). Are there any other examples of weeping and tears in the Bible that are striking to you?

Consider Heb. 5:7. At what points in His life and ministry did Jesus weep? Are you compelled by His example?

I RESOLVE TO RESPOND

Is there any way in which you have choked back your tears in prayer? Is the Lord speaking a fresh release to your heart in this area? Express to Him the desire and intent of your soul.

The inner chamber of prayer gains its impetus from the liquid power of tears.

33

For Group Discussion

CAN WE HELP EACH OTHER?

1. Do tears come with ease or difficulty for you? Do you feel free to cry before Him?

2. Tell of a time when you wept before the Lord, and you still remember that time as a significant encounter with God. Were your tears like "liquid words," expressing things your tongue could not express?

3. Are there certain things that you've found will move you to tears in the place of prayer? For example, meditating upon the sufferings of Christ's cross, and what He gave us through it? Or intercession for the lost?

WE NEED HIS HELP

Do you have a desire to follow William Booth's advice? (He said, "Try tears.") Let's ask the Lord to open the fountains of the deep within us. If there are any hindrances to tears, let's confess them and receive His help.

Notes

_____

_____

_____

_____

_____

_____

_____

_____

_____

_____

_____

_____

_____

_____

_____

_____

When it comes to the secret place, tears are either honest or they're absent.

34 The Secret of Holiness

"Lord, who may abide in Your tabernacle? Who may dwell in Your holy hill? He who walks uprightly, and works righteousness, and speaks the truth in his heart" (Ps. 15:1-2).

For Personal Reflection

I CHOOSE TO BELIEVE

Tell the Lord, "I believe I can live in holiness, by Your grace. You are eager to empower me to live in Your presence." With Jam. 5:16 before you, meditate in the authority you have before God in prayer because you live in the holiness of His presence.

I DESIRE TO UNDERSTAND

Read Ps. 51 in light of verse 11, where the Spirit is first called the "Holy Spirit." In this Psalm, David is returning to holiness. What steps do you see he took to return to holiness? Put a verse with each step you cite.

Read Ps. 15 and Ps. 24. Formulate your own personal definition of holiness. Holiness is:

How is it that God's disciplines bring us into His holiness (Heb. 12:10)? How have you experienced this dynamic? Get ready to share this with the group when you come together.

I RESOLVE TO RESPOND

Consider Col. 1:9 prayerfully. How are you determining to walk in the coming days, by His grace, so that He will reveal His will to you?

I am holy only to the extent that I abide in His holy presence.

34

For Group Discussion

CAN WE HELP EACH OTHER?

1. The author uses the expression, "Happy holiness." What images does that expression stir up for you?

2. Once you've known the intimacy of holiness, you realize that nothing is worth losing it. Is there any one thing that primarily hinders you from holiness? Do you have the courage to share it with the group? (Unless it's inappropriate to share in your group context.) How is God motivating you to overcome?

3. Share with your group any way in which you have experienced the dynamic of Heb. 12:10—how God's disciplines have helped you to perfect holiness.

WE NEED HIS HELP

Having shared our fight for holiness, let's pray for one another. Pray specifically for someone else in the group. Believe that grace is being released to that person as you contend in the Spirit on his or her behalf.

Notes

_____
_____
_____
_____
_____
_____
_____
_____
_____
_____
_____
_____
_____
_____
_____
_____

Holiness has to do with proximity to the throne.

35 The Secret of Buying Gold

"I counsel you to buy from Me gold refined in the fire, that you may be rich" (Rev. 3:18).

For Personal Reflection

I CHOOSE TO BELIEVE

Tell the Lord you are inviting His fire into your life because you believe that His refining fire will produce Christlikeness in your life. With fullness of faith, ask Him to baptize you with the Holy Spirit and with fire (Matt. 3:11).

I DESIRE TO UNDERSTAND

Read Chapter 35 carefully again, and then write out in your own words how we buy gold in the fire.

There is no cheap way to become more Christlike. When something is bought, one thing is lost while another thing is gained. When we buy Christlikeness in the fire, what are some of the things we lose? What is the pricetag? Can you find any supporting Scriptures for your answers?

I RESOLVE TO RESPOND

Tell the Lord that He is your "pearl of great price," and that you are willing to sell all in order to gain Him (see Matt. 13:45-46). How are you setting your will to respond when His fires reveal areas of darkness in your heart?

The gold we buy is called Christlikeness.

CAN WE HELP EACH OTHER?

1. Discuss this phrase, "The secret place is God's ATM." How can we use the secret place to access the gold of the Kingdom?

2. What are some ways we can think we are rich, when in fact we are poor (Revelation 3:17)?

3. Can you tell of an experience in the last week in which God's word "read your mail?"

4. Is the last paragraph on page 142 true? Can you testify that the Lord has been using this study to change you? Have you been growing in Christlikeness in recent weeks? Tell us what God is doing in you.

WE NEED HIS HELP

Let's call upon God's fire to come and rest upon us all. You may want to pray some Scriptures over each other—for example, Jesus said, "I came to send fire on the earth'" (Luke 12:49). A prayer: "Lord, You came to send this fire—now send it! Cause this fire to come and rest on each of us, Lord, even as it rested upon each believer on the Day of Pentecost (Acts 2:3)."

Notes

_____
_____
_____
_____
_____
_____
_____
_____
_____
_____
_____
_____
_____
_____
_____

Godly character is not given to us; we buy it.

The Secret of Inviting His Gaze

"His countenance beholds the upright" (Ps. 11:7).

For Personal Reflection

I CHOOSE TO BELIEVE

Do you believe that, as His child, His eyes are upon you for good? Meditate in Gen. 6:8; 2 Chr. 16:9; Ps. 34:15. Write your belief in the tenderness with which God looks upon you.

I DESIRE TO UNDERSTAND

Look carefully at Isa. 66:2, using whatever study tools you have. Using cross references, write out what it means to be poor; to be contrite (smitten of heart); to tremble at His word. What part of this verse means the most to you today?

Look at all the occurrences of the word "eyes" in the Song of Solomon. What role does the locking of our gaze have in our relationship with our Beloved?

I RESOLVE TO RESPOND

Determine to paint on your chest the largest bull's eye you possibly can. What can you do to get His full attention? How can you invoke the strength of His direct gaze? Write here the resolve of your heart.

If He likes you, He looks at you.

For Group Discussion

CAN WE HELP EACH OTHER?

1. Have you ever felt like Job in Job 7:17-20? Or like David in Ps. 139:23? Have you felt schizophrenic between the two? How did you walk out with God the seeming paradox?

2. After reading this chapter, do you find yourself wanting to invoke God's gaze? Or are you apprehensive? Talk about it.

3. Are you thankful for the fact that God is watching you? How do you feel about that? Do you wish you could hide at times? How can we get to the place where we view His constant surveillance as a token of His abundant mercy?

WE NEED HIS HELP

With the assurance of Jer. 24:6 before us, let each one express his or her own prayer to God—aloud, in the hearing of the group. We can do this in a circle, and then the leader can close in prayer.

Notes

_____

_____

_____

_____

_____

_____

_____

_____

_____

_____

_____

_____

_____

_____

_____

_____

Eyes locked, hearts burning...this is the secret place.

37 The Secret of the Cross

"And he who does not take his cross and follow
after Me is not worthy of Me'" (Matt. 10:38).

For Personal Reflection

I CHOOSE TO BELIEVE

The cross is the most extravagant way to say, "I love you." Will you believe that your cross is His invitation to an everlasting love? Take up your cross in faith. Tell Him what you believe about this cross.

I DESIRE TO UNDERSTAND

Consider 1 Pet. 4:19. What do you believe it means to suffer "according to the will of God?"

Pursue further the declaration of this chapter that the cross is the place of the highest intimacy. Which Scriptures can you find to support the truth that the taking up of one's cross is the greatest way to give one's love to Christ?

In what ways do you see Ps. 91:1 pointing to the cross of Christ?

I RESOLVE TO RESPOND

Meditate in Heb. 12:2. Decide by God's grace to endure the cross. Fasten your eyes upon Jesus, and give Him your love. Whisper to Him the passionate resolve of your heart to follow Him even unto death.

The cross's shadow is the saint's home.

CAN WE HELP EACH OTHER?

1. In the cross we say to our Lord, "This is how much I love You." Is this a new idea for you, to see the cross as a means of expressing the full intensity of our love? Does this change how you view suffering?

2. The chapter closes with the seven sayings of Jesus on the cross. Which of these seven sayings is most gripping to you right now, in terms of your own heart's cry to God?

3. God is raising up a generation today who are so willing to lay down their lives that they are even preparing themselves emotionally for the possibility of martyrdom. Are you prepared to be a martyr for the Lord? Is there any way in which you are extravagantly laying your life down for Him today?

WE NEED HIS HELP

We need His grace to say yes to the cross and to persevere through the suffering of the cross to the end. In what way is the cross applicable to your life right now? Is there any way in which you are suffering? Let's call upon the Lord for grace—not only to endure the cross, but also to uncover the extravagant intimacy that is available to us in the place of suffering.

Notes

_____

_____

_____

_____

_____

_____

_____

_____

_____

_____

_____

_____

_____

_____

*In our daily pilgrimage to the secret place, we wrap ourselves around
His rugged tree, gaze upon His wounds, and once again die to ourselves.*

38 The Secret of Rest

*"And He said to them, 'Come aside by yourselves to
a deserted place and rest a while'" (Mark 6:31).*

For Personal Reflection

I CHOOSE TO BELIEVE

Our chapter reads, "God can empower us to be more effective in 23 hours of Spirit-filled service than the 24 hours that the world has without His indwelling presence." Do you believe this? Express to God your confidence.

I DESIRE TO UNDERSTAND

Study Heb. 4:1 and its context carefully. What exactly is the rest that is available to us? What is so important about it that we should fear lest we fall short of it? What must we do to enter it?

Using your concordance to research "Sabbath," look at some of the Old Testament Scriptures that point to the purpose of the Sabbath (include Ex. 31:13). How do these principles relate to our rest?

I RESOLVE TO RESPOND

Are you willing to work hard to find God's rest (Heb. 4:11)? Write down what you're wanting to pursue in God regarding rest.

The Sabbath is to the week as the secret place is to the day.

38

For Group Discussion

CAN WE HELP EACH OTHER?

1. Have you experienced a time when spending time in the secret place actually increased your productivity that day? Tell us about it.

2. Is your secret place truly a respite and rest, or is it something at which you labor and strive? If it's the latter for anyone in our group, what can we do to turn that around?

3. Even other world religions practice meditation as a means of relaxation and renewing. Have you found your prayer life to actually help reduce your stress levels? In what ways?

WE NEED HIS HELP

Have each one in the group talk about his or her stress levels. What are the major contributors to each one's stress? Then let's pray for one another. Ask God to bring each one of us into the fullness of His rest. "Teach us this secret, Lord!"

Notes

_____

_____

_____

_____

_____

_____

_____

_____

_____

_____

_____

_____

_____

_____

_____

_____

What could be more energizing in the course of a busy day
than to stop and gaze upon the glory of His enthroned majesty?

The Secret of Pursuing True Riches

"Therefore if you have not been faithful in the unrighteous mammon, who will commit to your trust the true riches?"" (Luke 16:11).

For Personal Reflection

I CHOOSE TO BELIEVE

Do you believe that the greatest riches are to be found only in the pursuit of the knowledge of God? Tell the Lord that you believe all wealth is bound up in Him, and that He has changed your heart so that you might value eternal riches above all perishable riches.

I DESIRE TO UNDERSTAND

Take some time to peer into 2 Cor. 4:6-7. Do you agree with the author's interpretation of what the treasure is? What is the main word to be emphasized in verse 6? Some think it's the word "knowledge" that is being emphasized, do you agree?

Looking at Luke 16:11, what do you see as the link between faithfulness in financial steward-ship and being entrusted with the true riches of the knowledge of Christ?

I RESOLVE TO RESPOND

With Pro. 4:7 before you, tell the Lord what you're chasing after. What are you determined to get? Ask Him to seal this resolve with His grace.

The treasure is the knowledge of Christ.

For Group Discussion

39

CAN WE HELP EACH OTHER?

1. Why, in your opinion, is the knowledge of Jesus the greatest treasure?

2. Talk about Col. 2:2-3. What can we do to access these riches?

3. Look at Isa. 45:3. Is there any way in which the Lord has given you "the treasures of darkness and hidden riches of secret places?" Explain.

WE NEED HIS HELP

Make Ex. 33:13-14 your prayer together. Ask the Holy Spirit to help us make the knowledge of God our life ambition.

Notes

_____

_____

_____

_____

_____

_____

_____

_____

_____

_____

_____

_____

_____

_____

_____

_____

_____

_____

_____

_____

True riches are the wisdom, knowledge, and understanding of
God the Father, God the Son, and God the Holy Spirit.

40 The Secret of Beholding Jesus

"But we all, with unveiled face, beholding as in a mirror the glory of the Lord, are being transformed into the same image from glory to glory, just as by the Spirit of the Lord" (2 Cor. 3:18).

For Personal Reflection

I CHOOSE TO BELIEVE

Do you believe that Jesus is to be seen in every book of the Bible? Tell Him so, and tell Him how you feel when He reveals Himself to you. Tell Him that He is your fountain of life, your meaning for living, your universe. Tell Him your devotion to the secret place is a massive statement of faith in who He is.

I DESIRE TO UNDERSTAND

Look carefully at John 5:39-40. Herein lies the great key in approaching Scripture properly. What can we do to make our Bible reading a search for a Person rather than for principles? Be prepared to share your gleanings with the group.

Read through one of the Gospels (or get as far as you can), and make a note of those things you see in Jesus that are totally different from you. Do you find the quip to be true, "Opposites attract"? When you see Jesus in His unique beauty, does your heart begin to burn?

I RESOLVE TO RESPOND

If you have come to the Bible in the past for any reason other than to behold Jesus Himself, tell the Lord and repent clearly. Then set your face like flint. Determine that your pursuit of the Scriptures will be from henceforth a pursuit of the knowledge of Christ.

The Living Word desires to meet us in the Written Word, if we will but come to Him in the reading.

CAN WE HELP EACH OTHER?

1. When it comes to things like Bible reading, is it easy for you to function out of your head rather than your heart? How can we engage with God's word at the heart level? What has worked for you?

2. Share your answers from your personal studies: What can we do to make our Bible reading a search for a Person rather than for principles?

3. With Luke 24:32 in mind, can you share with the group a time recently when the Lord quickened a Scripture to your understanding, and it caused your heart to burn with passion for Jesus? What was the Scripture? What did He show you?

WE NEED HIS HELP

Let's ask the Lord to help us come to His word with the right motives and the right intentions. Plead with the Holy Spirit to rest upon the word and enlighten it to our hearts. "God, give us a burning heart! Give us the knowledge of Christ!"

Notes

_____

_____

_____

_____

_____

_____

_____

_____

_____

_____

_____

_____

_____

_____

_____

_____

_____

*Here's the secret: Your reading in the word can be a dynamic
and living encounter with the person of the Lord Jesus Christ!*

41 The Secret of Standing

"And I saw something like a sea of glass mingled with fire, and those who have the victory... standing on the sea of glass" (Rev. 15:2).

For Personal Reflection

I CHOOSE TO BELIEVE

Do you believe that when in prayer and worship, you are actually standing on the sea of glass and gazing at the throne of God? And that all you lack is the ability to see it with your eyes? Write down what you believe about your calling to stand before God and minister to Him.

I DESIRE TO UNDERSTAND

Review Deut. 10:8. How does this Scripture delineate your job description? Or is there another Scripture that says it better?

It must have been challenging for Elijah to simply stand during the three years he was in the widow's house. Can you think of any other biblical characters who had a lengthy stint of just standing before God, perhaps even against their personal preferences? Jot down the name, the passages involved, and the main points of that person's life that speak to you.

I RESOLVE TO RESPOND

God isn't looking for your strength but for your availability. What are you determining in your heart that you will do to make yourself totally available to Him? Is there one specific thing you intend to do that you can write down?

*One of our prime responsibilities (and privileges!)
is to stand before the Lord to minister to Him.*

For Group Discussion

CAN WE HELP EACH OTHER?

1. Let's ask the question in the group: Are you between assignments? If so, has this chapter helped you to know how to stand in this season of seeming inactivity?

2. What kind of spiritual warfare have you encountered when you set your heart to stand before God?

3. Are you more comfortable with "doing" or with "being"? (That is, with doing good works for the kingdom, or with just being in His presence?) How has God challenged your comfort zones and sought to broaden you out?

WE NEED HIS HELP

Is there anyone in our group who is in a season of "just standing"? Or perhaps you know you need to stand, but you don't know how to do it, or may feel too weak to persevere. Let's minister to these individuals, and believe for God to grant them the understanding, wisdom, and grace to be resolute and unmoving through this particular season.

Notes

_____
_____
_____
_____
_____
_____
_____
_____
_____
_____
_____
_____
_____
_____

"Don't just do something, stand there!"

42 The Secret of Bodily Light

"If then your whole body is full of light, having no part dark, the whole body will be full of light, as when the bright shining of a lamp gives you light" (Luke 11:36).

For Personal Reflection

I CHOOSE TO BELIEVE

Declare: "I believe that the light of God—filling my mind, soul, spirit, and body—has the power to change every atom of my being." Write down how you believe you can pursue this reality in the secret place.

I DESIRE TO UNDERSTAND

Study Luke 11:33-36. Write down the things you're seeing about this passage. How is your eye the lamp of your body? What does it mean to have a good eye? A bad eye? What are the benefits of a body full of light?

Connect this truth with Job 31:1. How significant was bodily light in Job's destiny?

Rev. 3:18, what do you think it means to anoint your eyes with salve?

I RESOLVE TO RESPOND

Are you intent upon getting your whole body full of light? Write down how important this is to you, and what you are purposing to do about it.

When the body is full of light, bodily sins lose their power over us, and we walk in a fantastic dimension of victory.

CAN WE HELP EACH OTHER?

1. Is the idea of having light in your body an idea that is rather new for you? Let's talk about this, from Luke 11:33-36. What does it mean to have your body full of light? What are your questions? What are your insights?

2. Let's talk about bodily sins. What have you found to be your most successful pathway to victory over bodily sins?

3. Got any suggestions for keeping our eyes on the holy and away from the unholy?

WE NEED HIS HELP

We're going to ask God, in humility, to help us fill our bodies with light. Let's ask Him to teach us, to show us the way. "Lord, cause Your word to light up my whole life! May so much light dwell in me that all bodily sins will lose their power." May darkness be gone from us, and may we adopt new patterns of living that keep the light burning strong. Let's ask these things together, fervently.

Notes

_____
_____
_____
_____
_____
_____
_____
_____
_____
_____
_____
_____
_____
_____
_____
_____
_____
_____

As we apply ourselves to God's word in a disciplined and focused way, our eye will slowly begin to heal and clear up and will begin to allow the light of Christ into our bodies.

The Secret of Just Loving Him

"Because he has set his love upon Me, therefore I will deliver him" (Ps. 91:14).

For Personal Reflection

I CHOOSE TO BELIEVE

Do you believe, in those seasons when all you can do is love Him, that love is enough? Do you believe that love is the most powerful force in the universe? Tell Him so.

I DESIRE TO UNDERSTAND

Look at Pro. 30:15-16. The fire of love never says, "Enough!" God's love is always searching for more of our hearts. Consider how His fire is always wanting more of You, and how your fire is always wanting more of Him. Make a note of the things you're seeing.

What are some of the scriptural promises to those who love God? Note the reference, and the promise.

What role does singing have in our giving of our love to Jesus? Which supporting Scriptures can you find?

I RESOLVE TO RESPOND

Spend some time right now simply in loving Him. Put all else aside and just give Him your love. Look for fresh ways to articulate your passion. Say it with the entirety of your passions and emotions. Tell Him that you're in this thing for love. And that's the way it's always going to be for you.

When you simply release your love to your Lord, you are stepping into the dimension where God works on behalf of His loved ones.

For Group Discussion

43

CAN WE HELP EACH OTHER?

1. Has there ever been a time in your life when the only prayer you could muster was, "I love You"? Tell the group about it. How strong was your sense of intimacy in that period?

2. For those in the group who have children, tell the others how you enjoy it when your children are affectionate with you. Make the connection to your relationship with your heavenly Father.

3. What does it mean to be rooted or established or grounded in love? How strongly rooted do you feel, in His love? Do you ever have times when you struggle, because of your circumstances, to love God with an abandoned heart?

WE NEED HIS HELP

Let's ask the Lord to make love the number one motivator in our secret place relationship with Him. May love outstrip every other motivator! But since our love is a response to His love, we need His help. Ask for His love to overwhelm and fill each one. Cry out for grace to "just love Him." Pray for those who struggle to love.

Notes

_____

_____

_____

_____

_____

_____

_____

_____

_____

_____

_____

_____

_____

_____

_____

_____

Love is the primary staple of the secret place.

44 The Secret of Being Known

"But if anyone loves God, this one is known by Him" (1 Cor. 8:3).

For Personal Reflection

I CHOOSE TO BELIEVE

Do some personal inventory right now. Do you believe that God knows you? Why? Declare your humble confidence in God's acceptance of you, and of your total sincerity before Him.

I DESIRE TO UNDERSTAND

Look at a couple instances where Jesus rebuked the disciples. What evidence do you see that He totally knew their motives, so He was able to correct them in a way that called them higher rather than shutting them down?

David said that he was known by God, and He invited God to know him even more (Ps. 139:1, 23). Using these verses, as well as Jer. 12:3 and John 1:48 and any others you find, list the benefits of being known by God.

I RESOLVE TO RESPOND

Pull back the veil from before your heart right now, and give every part of your heart to Him. Is there any part that you've withheld from God? If so, determine to receive the grace to give it all to Him. Whisper your passionate cry, "Know me, Lord."

*His acceptance is so incredible that it inspires me to open
every single crevice of my heart to His loving eyes.*

For Group Discussion

44

CAN WE HELP EACH OTHER?

1. "What must I do to be known by God?" How would you answer that question?

2. Have you inwardly feared if God truly saw who you were in the recesses of your heart, that He would reject you? Or do you really believe that He accepts you fully in the midst of all your struggles? Has this empowered you to search for more ways to disclose yourself to Him?

3. The Bible uses the word "to know" as descriptive of the marital union (e.g., Gen. 4:1). Intimacy is found in giving ourselves totally to another. How can we give ourselves even more fully to God, to know Him and be known by Him, in order to know the greatest intimacy?

WE NEED HIS HELP

Let's believe the assurance of 1 Cor. 8:3, "But if anyone loves God, this one is known by Him." Pray for anyone in the group with doubts or struggles. Express verbally to Him the parts of your life that you are laying open to His scrutiny: your body; your soul; your mind; your fantasies; your thoughts; your desires; your aspirations; your priorities; your career; your affections; your amusements; your spending practices; etc. Be specific regarding how you want to be known by Him.

Notes

The secret place is no place for secrets.

45 The Secret of Intimacy First

"I'm calling you back to your first love" (see Rev. 2:4).

For Personal Reflection

I CHOOSE TO BELIEVE

Pray these statements to the Lord: "I believe that love must be the primary motivating force in my life. Love for God must be foremost in my soul. Intimacy with Jesus is the highest priority of my life." (add your own convictions)

I DESIRE TO UNDERSTAND

Look at Matt. 22:37-38. What does the context reveal about these verses? What is the Lord showing you about the greatness of the first commandment?

Consider the wine of His love (Song 1:2) versus the wine of ministry. How is it that each is intoxicating and inebriating? What is God speaking to you personally about this? Which do you find more intoxicating?

Look up the "one thing" verses on page 182, and study them in their context. Write down the things the Lord is showing you.

I RESOLVE TO RESPOND

Are you returning to your first love? Are you determined to not only recover that fire of intimacy, but to nurture and sustain and guard it? How would you express this resolve?

It's the first commandment in first place, the pursuit of a loving relationship with our dazzling Bridegroom.

CAN WE HELP EACH OTHER?

1. Talk about how God made us. He made us lovers. He made us to work best when love is our primary motivator. How have you seen this principle at work in your life? Got a success story? A story of a failure?

2. "You can't garner intimacy on the run." How do you feel about that statement?

3. Has God ever starved out your fulfillment in your labors or ministry? Or possibly even removed your ministry? Tell us about it (without spilling unnecessary details about others). What was He wanting to change in you?

4. Are you ever relieved when your prayer time is over? Have you ever felt regret when you had to leave the secret place?

WE NEED HIS HELP

Let's each answer this soul-searching question, "Is there any way in which I have lost something of my first love for Jesus?" Let each one pray out as he or she desires. Let's all of us return to the Lover of our souls today.

Notes

_____

_____

_____

_____

_____

_____

_____

_____

_____

_____

_____

_____

_____

_____

_____

*By the time He is finished in our lives, we will be lovers
who work rather than workers who love.*

46 The Secret of Bridal Identity

"Then I, John, saw the holy city, New Jerusalem, coming down out of heaven from God, prepared as a bride adorned for her husband" (Rev. 21:2).

For Personal Reflection

I CHOOSE TO BELIEVE

Pray these things until you own them: "I believe I am part of the bride of Christ, and that You are empowering me to relate to You as my Bridegroom. We're getting married! I am ravished with love for You. Your cross has captured my heart. I am Your bride. Yours. Forever."

I DESIRE TO UNDERSTAND

Look at Adam & Eve's wedding in Genesis, and then the final wedding Rev. 21-22. As the Bible's bookends, these two weddings depict our relationship to Christ. What significance do you see in looking at these two weddings?

Choose another famous wedding in the Bible (such as the story of Gen. 24), and note the things you are seeing about the wedding that is to come.

Find all the biblical metaphors you can that reveal our identity, such as army, temple, body, etc. Put a verse with each metaphor. Do you agree with the author that "bride" is the highest metaphor of our identity in Christ?

I RESOLVE TO RESPOND

Ask the Lord to settle forever the issue of your identity. Ask Him to burn something so deeply in your heart that you will never again go through an identity crisis. Are you resolved to continue to study the theme of the bride of Christ in the Scriptures until this truth of your identity is fully established in your heart?

The secret place is the king's chamber, the place where we nurture our growing love relationship.

CAN WE HELP EACH OTHER?

1. If you're a brother, do you struggle to see yourself as the bride? And if you're a sister, do you struggle to see yourself as a son? How do you see yourself as both?

2. For those in the group who are married, what experiences from your courtship and wedding make you think about the relationship we have with Christ?

3. Let's answer the question in the book, "Do you ever waste time with the Lord?" (Page 187)

WE NEED HIS HELP

Are you wanting the Lord to make you into a lovesick bride? In what ways do you still feel the work in your heart is incomplete? Are you willing to ask the Lord, in the presence of the group, to cauterize your identity as His bride? Let's invite His fiery love to continue to transform our hearts.

Notes

_____

_____

_____

_____

_____

_____

_____

_____

_____

_____

_____

_____

_____

_____

_____

_____

_____

He died to marry a beautiful bride who will walk with Him, talk with Him, dream with Him, laugh with Him, strategize with Him, and rule with Him.

The Secret of Clinging

"I cling to Your testimonies; O Lord, do not put me to shame!" (Ps. 119:31).

For Personal Reflection

I CHOOSE TO BELIEVE

With John 15:5 before you, express to the Lord your awareness that you are helpless without Him. And then with Phi. 4:13 before you, express your confidence in God's ability to fulfill His purposes through your life.

I DESIRE TO UNDERSTAND

Read John 15:1-9. In what way would you say a branch "clings" to the vine? When you view the branch as "clinging" to the vine, what truths do you see in these verses that apply to you as you cling to Christ?

Look at Song 8:5 and its context. Which words describe what "leaning on Jesus" means for us? For starters, "dependence" and "uncertainty." What are some other words that come to mind?

I RESOLVE TO RESPOND

Spend some time contemplating how you could cling more fervently to Jesus. How would this clinging relationship be expressed in your own life? Cling to Him even now for a few minutes in prayer. Make a note of what God is doing in you.

During crisis seasons, the secret place becomes our source of survival as we come aside to cling to Him and cry out for help.

CAN WE HELP EACH OTHER?

1. Have you ever had a time when you thought you were going to lose your mind, and when you turned to Jesus, He helped you walk through your season of vulnerability? Tell us about it.

2. Do you have a testimony of a time when you were especially vulnerable and dependent upon the Lord, and He demonstrated His strength through your weakness and did more through you than He could have done had you been strong?

3. Keying off the bottom paragraph of page 191, have you known believers who seemed very confident in their position, and ended up rejecting the very stone God was wanting to use to build His Kingdom?

4. What will it be like when we're together with Jesus in the eternal city? What will be the nature of our clinging relationship? When we think and talk about these kinds of questions, we're obeying Colossians 3:2.

WE NEED HIS HELP

We all want to depend upon Jesus for everything, but we often find it incredibly challenging to do so. What is your greatest struggle when it comes to depending on the Lord and clinging to Him for sustenance? After sharing, let's pray for one another.

Notes

_____

_____

_____

_____

_____

_____

_____

_____

_____

_____

_____

_____

You won't mind so much to cling to Him in public
if you've already been clinging to Him in private.

The Secret of Walking With God

"Enoch walked with God three hundred years" (Gen. 5:22).

For Personal Reflection

I CHOOSE TO BELIEVE

Do you believe that a walking relationship with God is within your reach? Tell the Lord that you believe this is His will for your life, and that you know He will empower and help you.

I DESIRE TO UNDERSTAND

Meditate in Gen. 5:22-24. What are the things about Enoch's example that are standing out to you right now? Do the same with Gen. 6:9 (Noah) and Gen. 24:40 (Abraham).

Look closely at John 15:15. What is the difference between a servant of God and a friend of God? List as many distinctions as you can uncover.

I RESOLVE TO RESPOND

Ask the Lord what you could do to take another step toward a walking relationship with Him. Wait on Him for His answer. Then write down how you purpose in your heart to implement this step, by His grace.

The goal we're after is an everyday walk of
unbroken communion with our Lord and Friend.

For Group Discussion

CAN WE HELP EACH OTHER?

1. Talk about each of the elements involved in a walking relationship that are mentioned on page 194: companionship, dialogue, intimacy, joint decision-making, mutual delight, and shared dominion. Which of these do you feel is most lacking right now in your walk with God? Why might that be?

2. Discuss the statement, "God works with His friends." Do you agree? What does that statement trigger inside of you—i.e., how do you want to respond? Consider this statement as well, "When God has a friend, divine activity accelerates."

3. Talk about the three qualities God is looking for (page 197): humility, faithfulness, and loyalty. Do you see these as foundational character qualities God is looking for in His servants before He promotes them to greater service? Which of the three is your strong suit?

4. What was your favorite statement in this chapter?

WE NEED HIS HELP

What would you say hinders you most from walking with God the way you desire? Let each one offer his or her own prayer of consecration to the Lord (aloud, in the hearing of all). This would be a good time to confess an area of struggle or frustration and ask the Lord to supply an abundance of grace. Use the name of a Bible character in your prayer. For example, "Lord, give me a walk with You like Enoch had!"

Notes

_____

_____

_____

_____

_____

_____

_____

_____

_____

_____

_____

_____

When we walk with God, we enter the dimension
where God unfolds the secrets of His kingdom.

49 The Secret of Buying Oil

"'Buy [oil] for yourselves'" (Matt. 25:9).

For Personal Reflection

I CHOOSE TO BELIEVE

Tell the Lord: "Lord, I believe that getting and having oil is my responsibility. I believe You will teach me how to buy oil, because when You command us to do something, You always empower us to fulfill that command."

I DESIRE TO UNDERSTAND

Study Matt. 25:1-13 carefully. Make note of your own insights. When is the "Then" of verse 1 pointing to? Ten virgins: is the number ten significant? Why did the wise fall asleep? What do you believe is the eternal destiny of the five foolish virgins?

The overpowering message of the parable is, Buy oil! Can you find any other Scriptures that give a similar exhortation? Start with Isa. 55:1-2.

I RESOLVE TO RESPOND

Have you had a tendency to get just enough oil for the demands of the hour, without necessarily being prepared for the evil day? Are you ready to decide that you will buy and maintain an excess of the Holy Spirit's oil in your heart? Start today to implement your resolve by spending of yourself in the secret place until the oil is flowing.

When I am joined to Him, I lose my identity in the ocean of His greatness.

CAN WE HELP EACH OTHER?

1. Work to produce the best definition your group can put together for what the oil represents in the parable of Matt. 25:1-13. "Oil is:

2. If we "buy" oil, then obviously something is being expended in exchange for the oil. What is being expended? What is the price we pay to buy this oil?

3. Is it possible to have a personal ministry that is mightily anointed of God, and yet have your own inner supply of oil at a dangerously low level? What are the danger signs of that happening? Where will it end if we don't buy oil?

4. Talk about this idea: You can't get your anointing from somebody else's anointing.

WE NEED HIS HELP

Tell the group the main thing God is stirring in your heart, as regards buying oil. What is the number one thing God is calling you to do? After the first person expresses his or her heart, stop and pray as a group for that person. Repeat for each person in the group.

Notes

_____

_____

_____

_____

_____

_____

_____

_____

_____

_____

_____

_____

*The secret place is the threshold for resourcing the replenishment
you need to sustain through the dark night of Christ's delays.*

The Secret of Constant Supply

""Not by might nor by power, but by My Spirit," says the LORD of hosts'" (Zech. 4:6).

For Personal Reflection

I CHOOSE TO BELIEVE

A prayer: "I believe, Lord, that Your Spirit is the never-ending Source of life and strength to my inner person. I draw upon Your Spirit today. Fill me again, Holy Spirit. I am Yours. Fill me to overflowing." Meditate in John 7:37-39, and tell the Lord what you believe about the Holy Spirit as your source.

I DESIRE TO UNDERSTAND

Read Zech. 4 prayerfully. Underline the statements that strike you. What are you seeing in those underlined statements?

Viewing yourself as a lampstand with seven fires burning in your heart, if one of the flames is the fire of God's love, what might be some of the other six fires burning in your heart? Do you have any verses to substantiate your ideas?

The key to understanding Zech. 4 is in discovering what the source is—represented by the two olive trees. What do you believe those two trees represent? Seek the Lord in prayer for a connection to this limitless supply.

I RESOLVE TO RESPOND

If our pipes are clogged, the oil can't get to our flames. Have you got any clogged pipes? Ask God to do some divine angioplasty on your pipes. How can you apply yourself to enlarging your connection to the source of divine oil?

God has made available the opportunity to tap into a ceaseless supply of the Spirit.

For Group Discussion

50

CAN WE HELP EACH OTHER?

1. Have you seen leaders with an anointing to build, but who have been spread thin by running in a thousand directions at once? What have you learned from them? How can we build more effectively simply by drawing upon the power of the Spirit?

2. God is a constant Source—but for many of us, we feel like we "get fueled up" in a few brief moments each day, and then spend that fuel in the pursuits of our day. Many of us feel like we're constantly being depleted. What secrets have you learned about accessing a constant source in God? Let's share our frustrations and successes.

3. The chapter closes by talking about having a fire that is fed by an internal source. For example, when oil wells are set on fire in the Middle East, it's difficult to quench the fire because it's fed from an internal source (oil in the earth). How does this illustration portray the desire of your heart?

WE NEED HIS HELP

Tell the others in the group how they can best pray for you this week. Let's pray for one another—and then ask next time we're together how we're doing in walking toward a fuller life in the Spirit.

Notes

_____

_____

_____

_____

_____

_____

_____

_____

_____

_____

_____

_____

Nothing is more dangerous to the kingdom of darkness than
a man or woman who has found the unceasing wellspring of heaven's life.

The Secret of Abiding In Christ

"If you abide in Me, and My words abide in you, you will ask what you desire, and it shall be done for you'" (John 15:7).

For Personal Reflection

I CHOOSE TO BELIEVE

"I believe that the great secret of Christianity is right here, in an abiding connection with Jesus Christ. Because I believe in this so strongly, this is all my aspiration, all my desire."

I DESIRE TO UNDERSTAND

Choose one aspect of Joseph's pilgrimage and study it intently (Gen. 37-47). How do you see God preparing Joseph for a dimension of Spirit activity beyond anything he had ever known?

Can you think of any other Bible characters that God strategically guided through a season of difficulty in order to train and teach them to find the power of an abiding relationship with God? Write down the names of the persons, the applicable Scripture passages, and the main ways in which their life witnesses to you.

I RESOLVE TO RESPOND

Are you determined to put down deeper roots in God until you find the river of God? This will require lifestyle changes on your part. How are you resolved to be not only a hearer but a doer of this word?

The great condition to answered prayer is an abiding relationship with Christ and His words.

51

For Group Discussion

CAN WE HELP EACH OTHER?

1. Read the bottom paragraph of page 209 together. How much can a mentor help us in finding an abiding relationship in Christ, and how much must we discover for ourselves?

2. Joseph is the prime example in this chapter. What did you see about Joseph's life in your reading of this chapter that you haven't seen before? Has God ever used a prison sentence in your life to help you find an abiding relationship in Him?

3. Read the last two paragraphs of the chapter. Do you agree with the author's claims about an abiding relationship? Talk about the implications of such statements. What would change in the body of Christ if we found this?

WE NEED HIS HELP

Close by expressing the desires of your hearts to God. Tell Him how you long to abide in Him. Let the prayers be short, and let various ones in the group speak out their prayer as they desire. Each one might have several short prayers to intersperse into the dialogue with the Lord. Let your heart cry flow without inhibition.

Notes

_____
_____
_____
_____
_____
_____
_____
_____
_____
_____
_____
_____
_____

Whether it's flood season or drought season, there is a river available to the saint providing a constant source of divine life and Spirit empowerment. It is called "abiding in Christ."

52 The Secret of Union With God

"But he who is joined to the Lord is one spirit with Him" (1 Cor. 6:17).

For Personal Reflection

I CHOOSE TO BELIEVE

"I believe I am joined to the Lord, and therefore I believe that I am one spirit with Christ." Meditate in this truth until you have personal ownership of it.

I DESIRE TO UNDERSTAND

Ponder John 17:21-23. Are you able to form a mental picture of the union Christ is describing? How would you describe the picture you have of it?

From Eph. 5:22-32, what principles do you see that help us to understand union with Christ?

What do you think it means to be one spirit with God? If you have any fresh perspectives on Gal. 2:20, write them down.

I RESOLVE TO RESPOND

In prayer, see yourself joined to Christ. You are now one spirit. Your spirit is lost in His Spirit. Enjoy this moment of intimacy. Then resolve in your heart to return to this again and again. Ask God for grace to explore the vast frontiers of union with Christ. Your personal pursuit doesn't end here—this is but the beginning!

"When I am joined to Him, I lose my identity in the ocean of His greatness."

CAN WE HELP EACH OTHER?

1. Which statement in this chapter puzzled you most? Which statement impacted you most?

2. Did you ever have an experience where you felt especially joined to God? Tell us about it.

3. It's union within marriage that produces children. Would you say that it's union with God that produces the greatest spiritual fruitfulness? Can you think of an example, in your life or in someone else's, of how this might work?

WE NEED HIS HELP

Let's ask the Lord for such a passion for Him that, like Mary, we would be found looking, weeping, longing, yearning, watching for Him. Oh, that He would come to us, and that we might be joined to Him forever! Express the cries of your hearts for union with Christ.

Close by giving thanks for the blessing of spending these weeks together as a group, in His word. May God grant us the grace to fulfill every good purpose of our hearts formulated during this study. May the secret place be more than a phase, may it be a lifestyle. Amen.

Notes

_____

_____

_____

_____

_____

_____

_____

_____

_____

_____

_____

_____

It is in union with God that we find the greatest exhilaration, and
it is also where we discover the most glorious enticements
to explore the cavernous depths of God's burning heart.

Order Form
Books by Bob Sorge

	Qty.	Price	Total
BOOKS:			
SECRETS OF THE SECRET PLACE	_____	$13.00	_____
Secrets of the Secret Place COMPANION STUDY GUIDE	_____	$10.00	_____
ENVY: THE ENEMY WITHIN	_____	$12.00	_____
LOYALTY: The Reach of the Noble Heart	_____	$13.00	_____
FOLLOWING THE RIVER: A Vision for Corporate Worship	_____	$ 9.00	_____
GLORY: When Heaven Invades Earth	_____	$ 9.00	_____
PAIN, PERPLEXITY & PROMOTION	_____	$13.00	_____
THE FIRE OF GOD'S LOVE	_____	$12.00	_____
THE FIRE OF DELAYED ANSWERS	_____	$13.00	_____
IN HIS FACE: A Prophetic Call to Renewed Focus	_____	$12.00	_____
EXPLORING WORSHIP: A Practical Guide to Praise & Worship	_____	$15.00	_____
Exploring Worship WORKBOOK & DISCUSSION GUIDE	_____	$ 5.00	_____
DEALING WITH THE REJECTION AND PRAISE OF MAN	_____	$ 9.00	_____

SPECIAL PACKET:

Buy one each of all Bob's books, and save 30%.
Call or visit our website for a current price.

Subtotal _____

Shipping Add 10% (Minimum of $2.00) _____

Missouri Residents Add 7.35% Sales Tax _____

Total Enclosed _____

U.S. Funds Only

Send payment with order to: Oasis House
P.O. Box 127
Greenwood, MO 64034-0127

Name _____

Address: Street _____

City _____ State _____

Zip _____ Email _____

For MasterCard/VISA orders and quantity discounts, call 816-623-9050
or order on our fully secure website: www.oasishouse.net.

Notes

Notes

Notes